BOA
EDITIONS LTD

No Need of Sympathy

No Need of Sympathy

Poems by
FLEDA BROWN

AMERICAN POETS CONTINUUM SERIES, NO. 140

BOA EDITIONS, LTD. ❋ ROCHESTER, NY ❋ 2013

First Edition
13 14 15 16 7 6 5 4 3 2 1

For information about permission to reuse any material from this book please contact The
Permissions Company at www.permissionscompany.com or e-mail permdude@eclipse.
net.

Publications by BOA Editions, Ltd.—a not-for-profit corporation
under section 501 (c) (3) of the United States Internal Revenue
Code—are made possible with funds from a variety of sources,
including public funds from the New York State Council on the
Arts, a state agency; the Literature Program of the National En-
dowment for the Arts; the County of Monroe, NY; the Lannan
Foundation for support of the Lannan Translations Selection Se-
ries; the Mary S. Mulligan Charitable Trust; the Rochester Area
Community Foundation; the Arts & Cultural Council for Greater
Rochester; the Steeple-Jack Fund; the Ames-Amzalak Memorial Trust in memory of Henry
Ames, Semon Amzalak and Dan Amzalak; and contributions from many individuals nation-
wide. See Colophon on page 88 for special individual acknowledgments.

ART WORKS.
arts.gov

State of the Arts

NYSCA

Cover Design: Sandy Knight
Cover Art: Colleen Buzzard
Interior Design and Composition: Richard Foerster
Manufacturing: McNaughton & Gunn
BOA Logo: Mirko

Library of Congress Cataloging-in-Publication Data

Brown, Fleda, 1944–
[Poems. Selections]
No need of sympathy : poems / by Fleda Brown. — First edition.
    pages ; cm.
ISBN 978-1-938160-18-9 (pbk) -- ISBN 978-1-938160-19-6 (ebook)
I. Title.
PS3560.A21534N6 2013
811'.54—dc23
                    2013013076

BOA Editions, Ltd.
250 North Goodman Street, Suite 306
Rochester, NY 14607
www.boaeditions.org
A. Poulin, Jr., Founder (1938–1996)

Contents

for my grandchildren

Poetry stands in no need of any sympathy, or even goodwill. One acts from bottom, the root is the purpose quite beyond any kindness.

—Robert Creeley

I

One has to be able at every moment to place one's hand on the earth like the first human being.

—Rainer Maria Rilke

For, Or, Nor

For

"I'm leaving you," she said, "for you make me sick." But
of course she didn't say that. She *thought* the "for"; she admired
its elegant distance, the way it's wedged like an iron strut
between result and cause, the way it's almost "far," and dire

as a raised eyebrow. She liked the way it sounds like speaking
through a cardboard paper towel tube, using it for a megaphone;
not loud, but strong, all those compacted years shoving
out the other end, as if she were certain she wanted to be alone.

Or

The first four bars of Beethoven's sixth, the *Pastoral*,
repeat and repeat, always with variation: *or*, and *or*,
something to violate expectations, not fully antiphonal,
only an oar dipped into the measure to make an interior

swirl, pulling the craft slightly to the side, yet ahead,
still: little cupped trails alongside the mark where
the mind turned, questions were asked, and shed,
before moving on, nothing that can't be repaired.

Nor

As a flower sheds petal after petal, as further tests
strip away one after another of the last hopes for a cure,
as a person shakes into the waste bin all her cigarettes
and goes down the street not knowing who she is, the pure

air of saints is achieved by abandonment: Jesus in the garden alone, cold moon disappearing, Buddha at the morning star, mind emptied of its snarl of ignorance. Neither to harden against loss, nor to welcome it. To let it be who you are.

The Purpose of Poetry

1

The truth of it is, the stars won't give us any more
answers. We've sailed that way as far as we can.
Anyway, the Chinese discovered everything first.
What did it get them? The emperor Zhu Di
forced six million laborers to build the huge junks,
killing half in the process, most of starvation. The palace
burned; he renounced travel. They buried sixteen
screaming concubines alive with him when he died.
Add that to the horrors we already know, there's a kind of
trance, like watching TV, pixels instead of stars.

2

On *Law & Order*, the boy's father beats the soccer coach
to death because he thwarts his son's chance
for a scholarship. When we run out of oil, no TV.
Notice when the machines go out in a modern house,
it's like living in a corpse. Oil is heavier than poems.
Poems think that when the oil is gone, they'll sing
a ballad of when lights came on with a flick and you
could fly down the road so fast birds couldn't
remember you. Poems think they're on *Restore America*.
They'll scrape the ugly green paint off the fireplace stone
and bring back the superior life of the past.

3

Or they will stuff the terrible suffering into some
decorative urn that will ferment it into Beauty.
But the Big Bang is speeding up. All of this goodwill
is flying apart, and the poem is getting to be
about as sturdy as a spaceship made out of eyelashes.
It acts more and more like people trying to make love

after too much to drink, the climax always ahead
until the blank moment when it's gone.

4

Or like the birds outside our window. They think
the glass is the whole sky, some of them, but when
they hit, the other sky takes over, the one they never
thought of. I don't know why it's always the house wrens
and the sparrows, the least showy, the ones who live
in the Ninth Ward.* Poems keep trying. On TV,
I read the bios beside the pictures of those
killed in Iraq, seven or eight a night,
ranging in age from 19 to 45. I feel
the bios longing to be verses of an epic. In possibly
the oldest epic, Gilgamesh sits with his dead
friend Enkidu, whom he loves like a lover. He "veils
his face like a bride, paces around him like an Eagle,
like a lioness whose cubs are trapped in a pit." He tears
his hair out. Why did Enkidu die?

5

Because of a dream. Because he believed he would die.
This is the poem reminding itself how powerful
it is. Where do the dead sit? They sit
in pitch darkness dressed in feathered garments
like birds. What could be more like living? If Enkidu
could open the lid, living would be the very
pupil of his eye, his own TV screen. Captain Kangaroo
is dead, Mr. Green Jeans is dead. Mr. Rogers is dead.
Veterans with their quiet ways put on their old
uniforms and salute the flag, but the poem is pacing
like an Eagle, tearing its hair. "Why don't you just say
what you mean?" people say, especially the students.

---

* It's sad how even the most terrible things turn into footnotes. Students will read the foot-
notes before the poems. They will skip the poems.

6

But now the poem's occupied with the most seemingly
trivial tasks, like asking, "Where do the lost
shopping carts go? Where do the angels toss
their garbage?" And since there will be absolutely no room left
in the Cherry Hill landfill after 2012, the poem
is thinking it will clear its throat then, and try singing again.

The Kayak and the Eiffel Tower

The white sheet I remember, flashing across
the bed and I was watching my mother and the crying
and the bed disappeared and all was white
but it was not snow, it was my mind, and then, oddly,
she took us in a taxi to the movies, I think
it was *Ben Hur*. It was his postcard, now I know,
from that woman in the Philippines, back when
he was a soldier. All this, a movement
of shapes, nothing to hold onto. The kayak
is like that. It slides through the water and the paddle
goes on one side then the other, and there is the sway
of the boat and then the correction. It was
like that, and it was like the Eiffel Tower, all filigree
and lace, because I couldn't see anything solid,
but of course it was night and the movie was over,
I guess, but I remember the feel of her body,
her coat against my coat and the sidewalk rough
the way a child remembers the sidewalk: closer
than it will ever be again, grain after grain, and down
inside the grains, the press of earth that made
the grains, and the grinding that broke them apart,
and there were cracks in the sidewalk, and I swayed
a little as if I were in a kayak, not breathing but
sliding through with my mind so far away it was
on a lake, far out, and the shore wasn't the wool coat
my mother wore, not the coat, not anywhere.
And where was my father? Home, maybe, while
all this was rising from the bottom like a log, or a huge
gar, all the way to the top of the Eiffel Tower, while
my kayak dreamed its way off into some other story.

Bird's-Eye View

Even after the war, things went on
lockstep, our house in Terry Village one of
a hundred shotgun army barracks dragged
into place. We had one-fourth of one, thin-
walled, set up for GIs coming back
to school. And a great mud-puddle
out front, children eddying between
buildings looking for something
to do, digging under the 2 by 4 porches,
mothers on blankets drying their hair
under clotheslines, fathers tossing
cigarettes into brave patches of grass.

So my father made me wooden stilts
to lift me momentarily up, a bird's-eye
view. Not that he cared a whit for a moral.
But it was a simple spring morning,
dewy, spider-webby, and I was drifting
around in the new air, Saturday laid out
like a prize. I only remember mud-ruts,
the quiet, the way beginning took over
as if *of course*, which did, of course,
become the moral, if I had known then,
which was that tactics were never
necessary, only the wavering lifting,
and also the close literal examination
of beetles and pillbugs, in the face of
their brittle desire to remain obscure.

Sugar, Sugar

It was the trees, their amazing xylem and phloem.
It was the paper-thin cambium layer that made both wood and bark.
It was the leaves that took in carbon dioxide, released oxygen,
and sent the sugars down. It was the sugars, for sure, that ran
everything, the result of all that tossing around, that sucking in
rain, that fluttering evaporation. It was my first Pepsi, its sugar-
fizz, and the frozen orange clouds of the Dreamsicle, the slow
caramel centers of the Milky Way, the pure refined sugar
of them, concentrated, lighting up my body, for I was then
growing like a tree, wanting to get somewhere fast. It was my
mother and my father, the parts of me pushing and pulling,
the strain, the gathering into a bud, into the breast-buds,
into the flowering, the sugary colors of my flowering,
the Cover Girl Hot Pink lipstick, the henna hair rinse, staining
my fingertips red. It was so far away, so far from the tip
of a tree to the ground, yet the waters traveled through the narrow
tubes and arrived from roots and leaves, and the trunk slowly
thickened with its quiescent heartwood that shored up
all the rest, that was, really, quite finished with all the rest,
that let itself be wrapped by the sugar-hyped layers, so it could
think. It was not really thinking. What was it doing,
not bothering to call itself happy or sad?

My Father and Hemingway Go Fishing

Both of them would rather fish alone, but Hem asks
about the good spots here in the Antrim Chain,
a few miles from Walloon, so my father gets up
way before dawn, before he is my father, and rows
to the Ellsworth bridge where Hem is already
fiddling with his canvas pack. My father says get in.
This is the double-oared rowboat, so they both
row, *ker-flunk, ker-flunk*, oars in the locks in the dark.
They row through Benway, Wilson, the Green River.
Nothing can touch them, no one is up. One war
is over and another has not begun. When the sky
lightens, they can see each other, outline first,
both of them strong-jawed, dark, gorgeous,
but Hemingway does not know he is Hemingway
and my father does not know he is my father.
They scarcely know they are together because it is
the fish they want. It is better to have a third thing.
They are almost at the mouth of Six Mile Lake,
the blips on the surface, quick roiling underneath.
The bank is the cedar swamp with the cedars
slanted across the stream that in the stories are going
to stand for all the banks and all the streams.
The scholars will be climbing around, verifying.
They will say no, not this one. But there is the bottle
of grasshoppers, even dark ones, from a fire.
And their trousers are rolled and wet.
Who is to say that my father was not erased
from this later? Who is to say that they ever wished
to be together eternally? It was never anything
but the fish, the heaviness, the power, not to be
held, then held. Years after, even with me
in the boat, trying to cast my small line out, trying
to get one word of praise, it was the fish. I blame it
on Hemingway, and the cold water that pulled
the heart-blood inward, to steady its own small craft.

The Dead

The dead are disorderly. If they rot, worms;
if cremated, a waste of smoke. Maybe rot
is better. For where does fire-energy go? I see
energy transferred to worms and so on. But fire
speeds up molecules, then they slow down.
Worms can sometimes turn into winged things.
Good grief, I'm here on the dock thinking how best
to be dead! A dead fish lies on the lake-bottom,
white-belly up, quickly absorbed into the under-
world. The day's getting warmer. The day depends
upon the release of energy from the dead, whatever
has turned itself over to this rising. Triple layers:
earth, water, air—traversed only by those
who've taken the plunge, so to speak. I'm caught,
my foot in the bear-trap of living. Mother's grave
is sinking, the wood casket. We've betrayed her
once again. I feel her feeling, the suffering she
feels in there, the dirt, the disorder. She'll never
be smoke; she's heavier, sadder. I don't want to
talk about this. People who talk about abstractions
are like jet-trails that gradually disperse. Others
rot. They are loved by worms. Sad as it is, it's
more exact. There are bones, fingernails, hair,
and then the bones go, and the hair looks like dirt.
The dirt is happy and the body is happy
to be opened, after a lifetime of nail-biting. It loves
the way the air filters through, like carbonation.
It feels that it cannot feel. The not-feeling is like
not-being, only more so. Here come four
ducklings, there used to be five, still downy,
with their mother. I imagine the fifth one, the quick
turtle's jaw, the bloop under, the mother's wild
circling, then all settling, easy. The rest want me
to feed them. They bob in a nice neat row.

Pilgrims

From here my great-grandfather rowed out to modestly
bathe on the other side of the lake, change to his Sunday clothes
and row back for church, he of the ever-present vest and tie,

"representing the state of New York" even on the beach
in the photos which makes me think of the lost formality
of the everyday, the mannered manners that can, true, tie

down the soul, but on the good side be a vessel like a Hallmark
card for those unsure of what to say or do. Thank you and please
and all of us sit to dinner at the same time, using the butter knife,

the fish knife, passing the apple pie to the right, observing
the intricacies of crossing the silverware when finished, and
kneeling and prostrating and wearing black robes and white

and saying beads and creeds and gonging and chiming.
I think of chasubles and zafus, kimonos, rakusus, cassocks,
and Chaucer's pilgrims on their way to Thomas à Becket's shrine,

lackadaisically, his sacred remains safely buried beneath
the floor of the eastern crypt, a solid something somehow imbuing
all rag-tag, disparate, twenty-eight souls with a steady supply

of purpose and camaraderie, and I think of the tattooed and baggy-
panted hordes wandering through McDonald's and Radio Shack
looking for something to hold to, or, having given up on that, high-

fructose and iPhones revving up and tuning in to the higher
wavelengths that might have a clue about what to do next.
What was great-grandfather after, but grace in all its allied

forms? And Jimmy Swaggart, and priests with their sliding hands,
and the monk Chogyam Trungpa with his women and drink—
pilgrims all, with their lively stories along the road to pass the time

until they're done, and we're back on solid ground, this side
of the lake, where, church over and great-grandmother long dead,
great-grandfather headed out for hanky-panky with his sweetie-pie.

Roofers

Five roofers are wedging off the old,
scraping it over the edge. Great black birds
diving in front of the window.
In another place, a nail gun goes off in patterns
of four, sometimes five. They're nice guys:
one has a funny beard that sticks
straight out, one has a lip ring. One is pounding,
testing for rot. One is flipping sections of shingles
down; I hear them slap like clown's feet,
something out of Shakespeare. They know
what they're doing and they do it,
great rolls of thunder, the roof
of heaven cluttered with gods: Homer's
Tityus, Leto, Tantalus, the ones
who work the obscure jobs, who come
when called, the ones before Milton's great-
voiced dignitary, before Hopkins' rod-bearer,
the ones from the old days, from my old days,
when over my head, there was music
in the air, the pitch of my church-camp voice,
raised out of the heat and the breeze
and the sun on the spillway rocks, all of it
holding me in, as if I were in a shadow-box,
the kind someone looks through
a peephole and everything is 3-D, so the eye
is like the Important God. It fills me
with tenderness, the little world I had going on
inside, my grief that it was not the world.

Chipmunk of a Rock

1

I read, "The chipmunk of a rock dropped
      in a stream," before I saw "chimmuck,"
          the sound's exactly right word.
But the rock missed its chipmunk,
      the chipmunk that had depended upon it
          and held to it, perhaps, as part of itself,
so familiar it was with the contours, ragged edges
      and smooth surfaces. And the rock,
          feeling the cold for the first time,
feeling its crystallization as a burden,
      a weight headed for the stream,
          one giving, the other displacing exactly,
the geometry of cells arid as a dead planet
      chimmucking into watery space.

2

Among the magenta paintbrush,
      cinquefoil, and heather of Mount Rainier,
          I sat on a rise, and chipmunks emerged,
six of them. They came almost to my hand,
      little brush tails like surprised rudders.
          It seemed painful, to have to remain
on Orange Alert both for good and for bad:
      bits of sandwich dropped in the cracks,
          and the huge, shadowy forms inexplicably
arriving and leaving with some morality of their own.
      I had nothing to give, so I sat like a rock,
          except for my breathing, which I kept
smooth, for diplomacy. In this way, we set up
      our relationship, which I miss even now,
          its electric fragility, the meanings
that could shift second by second.

Year of the Tent Caterpillars

Tent caterpillars are letting themselves
down their almost invisible threads,
a horror movie of caterpillars, thickly
entwined on the walls and crushed into
a sticky sidewalk mass. They are down
my back, in my hair. I like it, though,
from up close when the sun's behind
and each one's tiny hairs glisten
like a teenage boy's gelled spikes. And
furthermore when I float in my kayak
over the ancient boat sunk beside
the dock and the tires fastened together
like ghostly underwater flowers,
all now encrusted with zebra mussels
(every stick, every chain and tire,
their tiny shells piling up, sucking out
the water's life until it's clear
as the Caribbean), I'm guiltily unsure
if I would change it back again.
As with the caterpillar's glistenings,
one scooch after the other, tiny body
waving along. As with the ones I've loved,
gradually going, those I hardly see
anymore, too, the veil keeps falling away
and I'm left with these worms feeling
for the sky, and whom do I turn to,
to say this is more than I ever thought,
and no worse than what it is?

II

Art, by its very existence, undoes the idea that there can be only one description of the real, some single and simple truth on whose surface we may thoughtlessly walk.

—Jane Hirshfield

Hare's Breath

We examine the toilet, hold the ball-cock up,
determine the flapper fails to fully fall.

We put a new one in, snip off the excess chain.
The tank fills only one-third full. We lower

the chain, change the settings on the dial,
flush over and over, studying the maddening

levels until the mechanism settles into
balance as inexplicable as this life we live,

machines coming on and going off, gears
spinning like dreidels on their perfectly honed

tips, a hair's breadth, or hare's breath, or hair's
breath, the metaphor long messed up,

all sense of origin gone, which no doubt explains
why we're floating, wavering, letting gallons

of water pass through, running up the bill.
I ask you, what volume can a hare breathe,

its tiny lungs pumping carroty air? How wide
is a hair? Furthermore, by what tiny margin

did the quarks and leptons have to increase
over antiquarks and antileptons to let matter

win out over antimatter, to bring us here,
to the flushing of toilets, filling of tanks?

Dancing at Your Wedding

I wish I hadn't danced like that, un-
dignified, wild, but consider your groom's
family, full press of uncles, aunts, parents,
generations of sticking together, then your own
scattered mess of faithlessness, and there
you are, father on one arm, me on your other,
two captive animals lured to the same pen.
There I am on the old VCR tape,
flouncing, you could say that,
into the reception with my new man,
your ex-stepfather crazily lurking
in the background. I'm wearing the filmy,
matronly mother-of-the bride-thing, grief
and joy thrashing in me like sumo wrestlers.
There we are, all layers of time
licensed to be here, and I am the smoke
of the speed of the rewind, in my smoky
blue dress among the calla lilies
and candles, and you a grand beaded
snowy island, a bell-voice at the microphone,
thanking us all, in general, and then I'm dancing
and dancing, stricken and turning, turning
my eyes. Imagine if Hades followed Persephone
back into spring and summer, not speaking,
sitting at a side table fingering the stem
of his glass, cupping its bowl, smiling
with his white teeth! Imagine if Rousseau
got up to speak of the goodness of the human heart,
and yours still bloody, the sweet smell
of a gardenia loud as a band
playing just under your chin.

The Heart Stops

The longest a heart has ever stopped and started again is 65 seconds, although some hospitals require you to wait five precious minutes to take the organs, but before his heart stopped, Linda asked her son David who had Down Syndrome, "Do you see Jesus? Take his hand, now, honey," words that fill me with tears for that walking forth past the 65 seconds, that coagulation into story of the whole life-death flux, the way it pushes my words aside the way we pushed the snow aside in front of the theater after watching *It's a Wonderful Life*, again, watching Jimmy Stewart, who like most of us hadn't a clue about what to do about anything until along came Clarence the angel, which goes to show if we follow our metaphors around, we learn something, and we keep on learning while the drones are dropping the bombs, and we are all learning to spell "Afghanistan," and we are all longing for a body for our sadness, but not one with cancer, which is what our daughter Pam has: something calciferous, like a concrete sidewalk under the tissue of our musings and our abstract drones, a sidewalk one hopes to divide into sections like a snake's reticulations, paragraphs which can be deleted, then radiated—a lovely sound, radiation, like angels—because common sense can't deal with sudden movements, the dangerously long gaps that open up, so the Sunday school piano works to fill the gaps.

The Chinless Woman in the Smart Park Booth

Her chin's collapsed like ripples at the shore, or a shirt
crumpled up at the waist. He likens it to this, or that,
the driver who doesn't want to become terribly alert
as he pays at the Smart Park booth. He's already sat

for hours on a plane and now is loose for home,
dragging these metaphors like tin cans off behind.
The proportion that makes for ease, the natural bone
that beauty calls its own—what else can the mind

do with its omission? The mind, we know
from several recent studies, prefers regularity,
likes it so much that a thousand people chose
a face made up of the average of a random sea

of faces as the one they most admire. Now this
transgression, the depth it hints at, the human fabric
broken down! How could one stand to kiss
that smiling vacancy? Once again grief has picked

a place to land, arbitrary, exact, scornful
of averages. The driver—who loves his wife and kids—
imagines the chinless boiling kiss, feels its pull
of absence, all the more for being sweet, rid

of self-consciousness. Something in him feels lost
as a child, his father angry, mother sad and far-
looking. He would like a certainty, not tossed
from one to the other, steering with radar. . .

I Take the Boys Up the Eiffel Tower

If we could see time, supposedly
it would look like a tesseract, beams sliding
along vectors, sideways and inside,
difficult as the leap out
from the Trade Center Towers—
you only get there by releasing a death-hold
on the last frame you've got.
                    We are on the way
up, late in the day, sun striping
the cross-girders, the boys and I
on the second-level elevator to the top,
crammed in like cattle. The higher we get
the more time's suspended, something to do
with Einstein, something to do with distance
squeezing out details that have meant
everything to us. The bees, for example:
what if we kill them off? And what if
there's nothing left for polar bears
to sit on?
            I tell the boys about Niagara Falls,
about sitting on the stone wall, my bare
little legs, knit cap, water pouring and tearing
below. "What happened?" they want
to know. "I didn't fall, of course," I say,
not remembering, really, only
the photograph.
            The rooftops of Paris fan out
below. "A giant spider web," say the boys.
Spiders, too, they'll be gone.
Meanwhile, they go on stringing
webs while our sky disappears behind
threads of lights, wind swaying
the platform. The boys' eyes get all
far away, as if the body could be emptied

enough to forget to die, or, at least
to fly through itself, god-speed.

Note to My Sister from Notre Dame

It didn't help that the boys are Jewish,
and the stone angels only clumsy halfway-
hoverers, not as smart as electrons,

quarks, or strings that turn like dazed
rubber bands in a breeze. It didn't help
that we'd walked all over Paris first.

Still, the rose window entered them:
a complication, a shattering of light.
Like the picture I saw of the inside

of the Hadron Collider in the Alps,
built to blast protons down to their
fundamental elegance, down

to the particle responsible for mass,
responsible for that cauldron of a window,
that scored and soaring ceiling.

There we were, our animal smallness,
our imagination turning in the distance
like a kaleidoscope.
                        What I learned

this year: you were propped in your
hospital bed, head lolling to one side,
one eye slightly open. We'd taken turns

for weeks, helplessly rubbing your feet,
machines spreading their arms overhead
like bony angels. Then we watched

your mind settle back into your body
and go to work again, inventing
everything, including itself. And where

was its source, the still surface refracting
the lights of consciousness? Nothing
I can say will ever name it.

My feet went flat on the stone floor:
it was a long way around the little chapels,
the saints with eyes like boys' eyes,

loving the subatomic, the ultrasonic.

God, God

We dressed for church. I had a white hat
and white gloves when I was fifteen, no joke.
You had to do that to show God you cared.

God's eyes were stained glass, and his voice
was pipe organ. He was immortal, invisible,
while my pantyhose itched and my atheist

father chewed his tongue and threatened to run
out the door but didn't for my mother's sake,
and she swallowed her fate, this marriage,

like a communion cracker, and my brain-
damaged brother lurched around the church
nursery, and my sweeter sister watched me

with huge brown eyes to see what I'd do next.
My God, why did I turn my eyes upward when
we were all there, then, in the flesh? I am so

sorry about *God*, sorry we fastened that word
to the sky. *God's* not even legal in Hebrew.
If you get the vowel caught between the two

consonants of your lips, it can carry you
dangerously up like a balloon over what you'd
give anything to be in the middle of, now.

The Puffball

Was beauteously, bulbously huge—redundant
as a luminous moon—puffed and balled,
seized by Uncle Richmond from the deep woods,
plucked with both hands and brought
to the doorstep for our amazement
and accolades, and to be sliced and fried,
tasting like nothing but slightly singed butter,
which we happily shared back then, several years
before he collapsed on the porch at 85
with a heart attack, having driven forty miles
from Petoskey home clutching his chest,
sweat streaming after the meeting
where the argument was made to inject
toxic wastes under the "perfectly safe" shelf
of rock to mingle in the underground seas and sift
slowly out to the Great Lakes as has happened
before. He stood and said so, hands shaking
more than usual, so that on the dark road home
he had to stop for a minute near King's Orchard
then drive on, legs finally giving way
on his own front porch, Lee luckily hearing
something like a branch falling, so he survived,
lean and leaving to range through the forests
after the fantastical and favor us with the tale
of it, again, or occasionally with the whole thing,
harbored and carried into our presence,
a careful joy, mysteriously magnified, come
upon as if the earth had started suddenly over.

III

I spoke to a psychologist, a man who has made his work and his theme the study of fear, and the talk went well enough until poetry was mentioned. Then, with extreme violence, a violence out of any keeping with what had gone before, the psychologist began to raise his voice and cut the air with his hand flat. He said, his voice shaking, that he had cut poetry out of his life, that that was something he had not time for, that was something out of his concern.

—Muriel Rukeyser

Reading About the Unsolved Murders at Good Hart, Michigan, 1968

—for Mardi Link

You get the vertigo of gruesomeness,
door still opening, mother, father, four children,

sprawled, unfound a month in the heat. Wall
of flies, bodies melted down to elements. Elemental

odor, as if one has tasted flesh oneself.
You wonder how there can be anything after that

but the willful separation into opposites—nice
cabin in the wildflower woods and the unspeakable

other. How did it get like this, passionate energies
locked up until they stank? For that matter, how do

all those women put on burkas and sit in the sun
by the hotel pool, dangling their feet and laughing?

The edges of their costumes are blowing in the breeze,
an initial disturbance. Let the door open, let the beholder

look closely at the result, and weep, let the tears leave
nothing for the flies, let the flies escape by their devious

paths, small black calamities. Like an artificial night
in there, it was. With the ladies across the way

playing cards, smelling the smell, their disgusted queries:
"Raccoon?" And the woods going on with their

greening: spring beauties and Dutchman's breeches
so tiny we could miss them, right under our noses.

Child Labor

Child labor is desperately sought by both the manufacturers
and the starving children. Morality is another one of those words.

Sometimes there's a haze of words, sometimes a fog. My breath
is one of the two. The palm of my hand is a shallow lake,

enough to hold stones and lose words in. The world is held
in God's hand. We sang this on the spillway at church camp

as fingers of water spread out below. True, the earth's crust
miraculously hangs on against the breath of all our talk, our tossed-

around ideas. Factory workers and children still forage in the dumps
at Phnom Penh, and under them, rats and bacteria eat away

at the garbage, and below everything, the earth's core swelters
in its own juices. Isn't it odd that we knew hell was down, heaven

was up, before we knew about the core? I would like to discuss
the consciousness that mumbles to itself so that it won't hear

the hum of sewing machines in the vast rows of warehouses,
and the children's pleas for bathroom passes. How consciousness

skips along on the level sidewalk of words as if it were headed
to a picnic. Heraclitus says everything is fire. We have lit a fire

in the barbecue pits, and the thighs of the large people who shop
at WalMart are on fire, but they can't help it. Things got heavy

so fast, to the point of combustion. It was the corporations who
got the children to make the T-shirts, it was the luminous ads

in the *Sunday Times* that sold the shirts, it was the carefully placed
words in the ads, God, we are all jabbering away while hell

cooks the hot dogs and heaven rains the iced sodas, and along
the banquette are the pump dispensers of ketchup and mustard.

Relationship Therapy

The young man needs his sleep. The woman wants
a word of love, a kiss. He turns to her, sarcastic.

The TV therapists take notes, express astonishment.
The camera's on the couple floundering in the quilt

somewhat self-consciously, in bed, their eyes
bright disks, like jack-lighted deer. We're headed

down inside to see what's wrong. The ocean at its
deepest part is warm and beautiful with hairy fronds.

Deep in the heart. Although, beneath the street,
blind pipes connect the noiseless streams of feces,

urine, tampons, condoms, remains of what was
wanted once, sent off to strain and settle, aerate, and

commit to soil. The heart's all give and take, Heaven
and Hell, we like to say, our thoughts enlarging like

balloons to lift us up or snap us down. We drift
so far away! What will happen to the couple? Will

they practice how to say the sweet things love
requires, to touch each other well? Will the endangered

Crested Shelduck live? Will monarchs fly through
haze and concrete fields to South America?

On nature shows, the close-ups come so close
monarchs obtain a stained-glass glow, fragile as

the soul, unable to survive alone. Our couple gets
an exercise to do, on camera. They have to swing like

circus acrobats, on opposite swings, then gauge
the perfect second to grab each other's hands, release

the feet, and trust each other's hold. This demonstrates
the need to synchronize, to make the most of time,

to feel how short it is. The swinging and the latching on
convince the body how the mind should act.

We watch this silly therapy, the couple who believe
in it, its wild exaggeration, the rocketing

and orbiting we like to think will save us from ourselves.
We know the camera's there, the audience of past

and future wait. The bedroom lights go down. Now
hands across the wide expanse of sheets. Whatever

do results mean now? Stem cells turn into anything,
given the chance. Drug companies pay a zillion bucks

to get results they want. What if he marries her?
What if they have four kids? Will the monarch get

to Venezuela? The panda mate in captivity? The mind
swings yes and no, grabs for the present moment,

makes up metaphors like crazy, a circus of them, links
unlike things in bed, to see what happens next.

Here, in Silence, Are Eight More

Night after night the photos of dead soldiers
go by on the *News Hour* like playing-cards while we drink

our wine, though we stop for that length of time, of course,
out of reverence, but it's not enough. The well of

how-not-enough-it-is is bottomless, deeper than TV. Even
if you track back through the Comcast cable, back to

the electrical impulses, you're not even close to what to do.
Not even if you end up on Main Street in Salisaw, Oklahoma,

and follow the 19-year-old into the storefront full of
uniforms, crisp, medallioned, follow not his vanity

but his hope, his longing for order, for the squared shoulders
of order, his wish for the vast plains of the world

to unroll at eye-level, so he can walk out into the particulars,
the screaming, the blood. Owen, Brooke, Sassoon: what

anthem for the doomed youth this time? His death rests
like a quarter in the pocket, a sure thing. Its arrival

is a few missing lines I fill in, wrongly, because
the mind does that: I have him watching in slow motion,

with love and pity, the flowers beginning to bloom
on his shirt, the sky closing like a book. Sadly, then,

he disappears entirely into my mind, his last breath
easing between my words. There was a book in his childhood.

No, mine. Ducks cross the road, a mother duck leads them
through traffic to the pond. The pages flip so that

the ducks seem to move. They slide into the pond
with the satisfaction of making it through the human

confusion. Our soldier floats like a duck. Like a night-flight
casket. In the photo his eyes, straight-forward, being all

they can be, float on the surface of a pool of uncatalogued
genetic material. One snapshot in time, his eyes were

like that, his mouth. He can't remember. He never was
like that. He was playing dress-up, then, hoping to make it true,

and did, so true no one could get in a word, in protest.

The Illustration

Linda came in silently from the hall—she raised her finger to her lips and her eyes danced.
"Hist, comrades," she said, "there is mystery afoot."

> —from a novel by Robert Ormond Case, published serially in *Country Gentleman*, 1936.

She's a pink rose, flounce upon flounce, the set table
behind her blanched. The brother, the father, all three
enact their miniature gestures, their signals, the way
the privileged do. Forever, the ancestors have kept to
their frames, forever the chandelier has blinked
its constellation, the chairs stiffened their backs. Forever
the white-haired father has presided over the plot whose
consequences will be amusing, will never cross the threshold
into disarray and darkness. Their little mystery is a slight
stirring of the air, a brushstroke. The world is made
of glass and whispers. You with your boots, you with your
hunger, clearing your throat, snorting like a cow, nothing
will make them turn your way. Nothing will stop their play,
even if you die, even if soldiers come and take you away.

Short History of Music

When I think of the taxi driver,
also I think of London's birds
who only sing at night,
the one silence left to be heard in.

It's the Muslim driver from Pakistan
who steers me two hours through traffic from Gatwick
to St. John's Wood where the rich Americans live.
His mother's ill, he says; they've brought her to London,
the father remaining. Remaining with his own
upholds him, he says, and I'm fingering
the deep gash in the upholstery; I'm down
to the steel. "We try to forgive,
Madam," he says, "but when Americans
burst down our doors with guns. . ."

        Birds live completely inside their song,
throwing it out at intervals like a plain chant,
clear notes, each a single insistence.
In the night it enters the consciousness
like a dream hidden under bed sheets,
or pressed to the pavement under the heaps
of garbage bags in the street.

A single voice, like the one Palestrina wrote in
to sing the scripture: all the others
in the background, holding their long notes.

Before him, Pythagoras and his triadic tones
gathering up our Western chords like small armies.
Even though others may call out while we sleep,
all we can say is "Sorry, sorry, sorry."

Big Bang

The whole blessed universe was steam
and density until the crucial moment
came, and *blam!* a billion billion different
ways to go, one of them this hawk, building up
tension for a dive. As when:

(1) a column of smoke breaks into chaos,
(2) you know you married the wrong man,
(3) in Casablanca, Rick sends Ilsa away,
to save the world.

"We'll always have Paris." Ha. Hold
one pose long enough, birds fly off branches.

The hawk barely shifts.
Somewhere below, a mouse, maybe,
holds perfectly still, feels the change of air.
It loves its life. The hawk loves its life.
The hawk loves the mouse. At the last,
the mouse looks straight into the eye
of doom, is eaten by its doom, becomes
its doom, no doubt is in love with it, now
that it's all doom itself.

It's the bipolar universe, off meds,
where all the excitement is. Ego, superego, id,
out to destroy each other, then growing all mushy
at the final moment when Good seems to have won out

over various Evils, which is an anagram for Elvis.
Elvis, had he lived, might have been like Mick Jagger,
still a bad boy at 63, but singing flat.
Watch him dance on the far edge, headed for
chaos. We're all quivering on a black hole's edge.

The difference between falling in and not
is one to the fifteenth decimal place, and
it does no good to hold your breath.

Memorial Day

The dead seem like holes in the universe,
each a random fuzz-spot, a sad little purse.

Cottonwood tufts are floating thick as snow
between these trees, lifting like loose souls.

One person would say mathematics, another God,
the way they float ethereally, yet each pod

responds to currents. (One slight draft, one bump
against the hypothalamus, say a bullet, or the lump

of a tumor, too much one way, a little confusion
of thinking, we fall.) All our mini-contusions

are gathering like seeds within a cloud of unknowing.
Under the circumstances, what to do but wing

along, try to hold the mind respectfully between
explanations like a rudder? Let the wind fling

us to the next hopeful span of ground, let
the dead bury the dead, let the rain forget.

Michigan

1

In L.A., I saw that too much sunlight made me nervous.
When my plane dipped beneath the Philadelphia clouds,
I sighed with relief, knowing I was ruined for the open
kind of joy, that I had grown better at irony. We moved
to Michigan so that I could think of summer as an exotic
land. I used to sneak through shortcuts between yards,
the backs of backyards. One tight spot you had to duck
through, under grapevines. You came up in a dank
grotto so close to civilization you could see cars,
but no one knew.

2

On the pinkie of Michigan, the lake effect makes
clouds until January and the sky clears
for a while, then the rain starts and summer comes
and is gone. You get that giddiness for a few weeks,
but never the sense of having been blasted open,
never enough to combust. Human flesh requires
extended exposure to 1,400 degrees Fahrenheit
in order to ignite. The human body, which is 85 percent
water, burns in a cycle of layer-by-layer dehydration
and ignition. Best to get out of there at the downside
of the cycle, before the heat dries out the next layer
of skin and the fire ignites it and this continues
until the internal organs are consumed.

3

I was lying on a towel on a creek bank in Arkansas
back then and it was so hysterically hot I married
the first person to come along. After that I was looking
for academic life, cooler climes. I had in mind

something like the brushstrokes of a Monet painting:
the water garden, the Japanese footbridge,
for example, where it is lushly summer but as if
it were a secret, a reflection of a person's idea
of summer. If you're in the middle of "real" summer,
where can you go from there? It's too hot anyway.
If you turn on the window air conditioner, you end up
sitting in front of it all afternoon. We had an air conditioner
in Little Rock that only worked when it was cool.
When it got too hot, it shut itself off. I would close
the curtains and keep the cool inside
but after a while even the dark didn't fool me.

4

I am not a tomato that ripens in hot summer nights;
it was not dark, but cold I wanted. I wanted to sigh,
"If only I lived in Texas, if only I could strip naked
without freezing." I love the subjunctive mood, its talent
at keeping out of the fray. It is like the telephone.
You call up and recorded phonetic elements combine
to make words come out as if on the other end
of the line a real someone has been waiting to remind you
your call is important to her and you should wait.
It is like my students whose grandmothers die
and die again, just before holidays. No ideas
but in things, but it's the ideas that pay off.

5

Oh, how can I live in Michigan if my sister's stuck
in Texas where the heat's in the danger zone, if dust
is thickening and crops are withering, if people
are walking miles across Africa? When will I tackle
the problems? I worry about that, but I definitely
eschew being one of those useful trucks going up
and down I-95 with their hot exhausts, the ones

I see from my creek bed, my grotto that isn't really
but I call it that. Eschew sounds like "It's you,"
or "a shoe," or "let's chew." I am sorry but I keep
following my nose, staying close to the ground. If only
I were picking up the scent. I am snuffling hopefully
through this lovely gritty porous Michigan dirt.

IV

Calm the heart's dark waters;
collect from deep thoughts
the proper names for things.

—Lu Chi

Pointillism

Before the camera,
there were portraits
and landscapes
to show how it was.
But that wasn't how it was.
It was a mass of molecules
like tadpoles in a pool.
No, it was the space between,
and the colors were only
light tossed through
the hoop of the eye
into the brain.
How it was, was nothing
you could name,
which is why
when, for a moment,
it came out, and was clear
to you, it was so dear.

The Grandmother Sonnets

Josh, 15

The grandmother collects what she can of the past, stows it,
jumbled, in an old bag she hasn't taken time
to sort. She wanders down streets you don't know
the names of. Even on the day of your birth, she climbs
through tangles, dutifully walks the dog Samson,
dumb lurch of a retriever, straight into the tiny clout
of two snarling pugs. Samson drags her along,
terrified and panting, back to the house.
Out there, a truck revs. She and the dog—the worse
for shivers, eye to dilated eye. Across town,
your mother's hormones are dilating her pelvis bones,
switching the new grandmother's life into reverse.
As on the elliptical trainer, the brief pause, then,
face forward, she's running backward toward the unknown.

Zach, 14

What steers the second grandchild—thin, small-boned,
blowing the trumpet while life grinds its gears
like a truck? The grandmother doesn't wish him thrown
to the gods of Art that require the shivering, the mere
skin's quivering molecules. She, too,
wanted nothing more than to be held. Apparently,
she notes, the basic structure's like this: a queue
of self-protecting petals, trumpeting pistil. One sees
nothing of the soft inside. What lies on the surface
tries to be bright as brass, a reflective door
against the other. She will never let the children
see what it was, back then, how she finessed
her rage, sent the grandfather away, how she adores
this trumpet, its wail like her own self back again.

Jake, 11

Harry Potter grandson, video forever blooming
in your round glasses, how can she find you, how dare
enter? She stands over, the awkward looming
of a grandparent, the useless gesture of ruffling the hair.
No way to revise the past, to travel back through
to your father, how she stroked his hair, small child
kneeling on her bed, sobbing for his father, who used to
lie on the floor and raise him on his feet, fly him, wild
with joy, while she sat knowing what this would come to.
Heart breaking, we call it, more of a steady muffled
truck-sound in the distance—deep bass, a movie sound.
How to comfort you for what you never knew—
how your father flew down into his books, the terrible
dark arts thundering outside the door like snowplows.

Noah, 10

The grandmother attends your Roman Carnival. You're
dressed as a physician, toga splashed with red
from cutting holes in the head—a Roman cure
to let the illness out. Your classmates have read
other tales: they stand, circled, at different addresses.
They tell her of gods and goddesses, food and drink,
temples and baths. Then she comes to you. She presses
the button at your station. She gives you a wink.
Which cure will she choose? She takes the hole in the head,
to let in light and stars, the galaxy of things
she's hoped to learn, the stretch of history from one end
of the room to the other. Now three gladiators: one dead,
the rest jab at shields. The grandmother's head rings,
but whatever bad stuff enters, can just ascend.

Max, 9

You and the grandmother build a house of snow,
exciting for you, come up from the South. You stare
into space. Minutes, blank. The grandmother knows
how you are. She tucks a random hair
under your cap. Something out there is lovelorn—
the whited-out sidewalk and sky. Something ignores
your work, weighs heavy compared to it, mourns
wordlessly. So thin you are. So many more
grandchildren, plus your father's grown children,
and grandchildren, even! The grandmother pulls your glove
back on, the one you dropped as if you could let go
as well of the crowded, mixed-up world, the din
that deafens your ears to the pure sound above
all that: your voice, delicate as snow.

Samantha, 9

The grandmother plays knights with you on a snowed-in
afternoon, looking for you where you might be found,
inside your toys. The knights come apart, fasten
with magnets. You take one knight's body, surround it
with five heads, thinking up a question. The legs, strewn,
answer that they have given up bringing answers.
One body with silver mail, one with gold, soon
interchanged. You tuck each of their dangerous lances
under the arm of the other, keeping the tips warm.
Love with a safety plan. Your curls fall across
the pieces so you can concentrate, the glitch in your brain
at war against confusing extra sounds. The swarm
of sounds in the grandmother's head, too—the lost
past. She strains to hear you over the cries of the slain.

Joie, 7

The child's serious brown eyes, full without prejudice.
Eyes like her mother's: part mirror, part well.
The step-grandmother flies to Oregon, not to be remiss
at grandmothering. Ah, a child can easily tell
the truth of absence! Here in the minivan's back seat,
they find objects out the window, beginning with letters
of the alphabet, in order. She keeps on, street after street,
to the tiresome end: good reader; speller, better.
Knows q needs u. Knows the rule that one parent
lives miles from the other, an alphabet to range.
The grandmother and the actual grandfather come
together. The grandmother's brought gifts: a sense
of continuity, of love. She's carsick. It's strange,
she thinks. Happiness is not a direct sum.

Rita, 6

The grandmother makes your mother cry even before
she's your mother. The grandmother objects to the name
your mother wants to give you: the ex-wife's, ex-adored
one's. But the difference between Rita and Rita, all aflame
then, becomes only inflection at last—one light
as ballet slippers, the other sounding into a well,
too far to see what it strikes. Look at you, feeding bites
of bread to the ducks, giggling. You cast a little spell,
do a dance on tiptoe, rattle the dock's molecules.
Ankle-high in the shallows, the grandmother feels the waves
swallowing in mini-gulps. The lake is sixty feet deep,
a half-mile across, sun turning the surface to jewels.
So as not to scare you, it is quiet about the way
it is going to rock every one of the grandmothers to sleep.

Casey, 5

Piano for pounding both black and white, cup
and stick for drum corps, lap harp for plucking out tones,
xylophone wall at the park for stroking the stones
to life: the song of Casey, wild to make up
something out of nothing, right foot in, right foot
out. Casey, singing in his booster chair, firing
bits of peanut butter sandwich into space. Stay put,
grandmother, a reverberation alongside, conspiring
against the sandwich song! She with her lead
feet sweeps up what has fallen. She is all for the dancing,
if it's old time rock and roll—its nice four-four
measures. She likes the way they plan ahead,
the way they let the past bounce along, advancing
only inside their exact, though passionate, score.

Abigail, 3

Is the grandmother's life generic, after all—the clichés
she's "spent a lifetime" struggling against? Her worry
over healing, over scars, nothing but the talk-show way
to say original sin? Here's Abby, all flurry
on her pink scooter, dragging her pink polka-dotted
rain boot, braking. Half a block behind, the grandmother's
mortality feels more like a fading, less knotted.
During pledge week, she watches, along with all the other
elders, the aged Motown singers. The theme
is death, start to finish. A lovely arrogance, legs
and arms and scooter, then a decline. It transpires
so quickly, the grandmother gets a little queasy.
She had something to warn about love, hesitates to say,
afraid to disturb the balance the wheels require.

Ribcage Heart

My heart, my
feather-heart,
my ribcage shadow,
my bone heart
my violin heart,
what do you
look like, tied
to me and singing
your one pragmatic
song? How much
longer can this go on,
after what I've done
to you, trying all
manner of romance,
trying to hook you
on it like crack?

Worms

Worms can replace parts.
They can restart themselves
if they're cut apart. And
the slime they leave behind
glues the earth together.
They have no eyes.
Imagine scrunching alone
through life, armless,
legless, and blind
yet so convinced
of your usefulness that it
makes some kind of sense.

V

I think I am probably in love with silence, that other world. . . . Silence which drowns us out, but also which ignores us, overrides us, silence which is doubt, madness, fear, all that which makes the language bend and slip.

—Jorie Graham

Building a Cathedral

In Barcelona, the massive gothic Sagrada Família sprouts
        its native-species gargoyles—lizards, etc.—according to Gaudí's
plans, an astounding city of stalagmites growing "from nature,"

as he said, even though he died in 1926, twelve years into it, leaving
        a three-dimensional miniature to work from, all based on
the golden ratio: arches like trees, columns like plants, windows

like marine diatoms. Meanwhile, my father has found that if
        he sets the microwave for 1:29, the rotation will stop with
the cup handle facing out so that it can be most easily removed.

Occasionally it takes 1:33, depending on the cup. He has calculated this
        carefully over a period of time, a timeless truth. He's 92
and has nothing but time, wandering around his nice clean retirement

cottage without his tools, his bicycle, his boats. Furthermore,
        he's managed to remove the point of a ballpoint pen cartridge
and tape it to another cartridge so that he can blow the ink from one

to the other when the point of one is stopped up. No waste there.
        He's using up his days organically. I wish I could go back
to Gaudí here, but my father's too compelling. How much longer

will I have him to show me what to do and not to do? His legs
        are getting weak although they retain the residuals of good genes
and a life of motion. He wouldn't call it exercise. He's found an exact

combination of kerosene and oil that keeps his Windsor mantel clock
        running and on time for about a week, after which the kerosene
dries up and the clock slows down again, not that it matters any more

or less than any other human endeavor, not that anything much
matters to my father anymore, which I notice is a frequent
condition of extreme age and makes me wonder if it isn't perfectly

natural to back out of life slowly, reducing our interest to the diatomic,
the minute minute. Even his sweetie isn't much to him,
demented as she is, but they sit every evening at his place, TV blaring,

and he puts his hand in hers. They don't seem to be thinking
of anything, not even the show, just waiting like Vladimir
and Estragon in *Waiting for Godot*. My father makes her lukewarm tea

the way she likes it and nods and says what's necessary to prove
he's there as she retells the ancient past again. On the phone
he tells me he'd rather be dead if it wouldn't hurt, or hurt

anybody. In the play, Godot doesn't arrive and the hanging-rope breaks,
and Estragon's trousers fall down, and they do it all over again
the next day. It's an important play. It shows us being us, although

it's not much fun. Beckett is an important playwright. We had to read him
in school. It was all true, but we were too young to care.
If we were born astride the grave, we were going to swing across

on a Tarzan-rope yelling and beating our chests. We were going to
build cathedrals and other stuff. Some of us did, some didn't.
This part is almost over for my father. When my Nana lived in Colorado,

where they moved her when Granddaddy died, she made a rooster
out of seeds in the Home Craft class. How stupid to end
your life gluing seeds to a board, I thought, but my mother hung it

on the wall where it stayed long after my mother's own death,
until my father sold the house. When we threw it
in the dumpster it felt, cruelly, as if now I could start over, really.

Felled Tree

Dear swollen-trunk maple, deemed
diseased by the saw-happy tree guy,
you who have stood silently, supposedly
slipping your ailment through your roots
to the neighboring trees, now fallen
full-blast down, geometrically down,
right-angle, then parallel at last, your flat-
sawn stump blotched with incriminating
evidence—you came and leafed
and are gone, and I who have grown old
in your lifetime, who intuited you rather
than knew you, felt you in my bones,
now feel the slightly thinner woods,
the hint of frailty. Scott the tree guy
has carried your 18-inch logs in his
red wheelbarrow and stacked them
for winter: a little Williams, a little Frost.
          Oh, tree, everywhere I look
I have to pledge reclamation, fill
the forest floor with ferns, mushrooms,
pine needles, and in the side corner
place the outhouse, practically unused
anymore, still in good shape, emitting
its rich human waste-smell, its wood-
smell, its few spiders climbing
their trellises with their sticky feet.
Oh tree, so much has been discovered
to fill in the space where you were:
seven new species of Philippine
forest mice, a new genus of blind
Bulgarian beetle, four new species
of jewel beetles, six of New World
micromoths. I have filled my notecards,
I have left the vertical space open

for the ur-tree, the canonical vision
that will take your place, even the stigmata,
your bulged and arthritic joints, the
whither of your leaving, the grand word
whither standing where you were.

Translation

The woman with the pale hair is signing
the poem. Not that kind of signing.
Her hands dip and flutter and hop
against the black backdrop.
Her mouth shapes emoticons.
Really, I'm not sure what
the mouth's for. I watch her lips,
the poem changed to hieroglyphs.
She makes her eyes turn off and on.
Keats could do no better. *Still*
wouldst thou sing and I have ears in vain.
Her face goes from happy to pained.
She is inside the poem where the birds live
with their hollow mouths.
I am watching her more than I'm listening.
The poem is not something she believes.
It has sprouted on her like leaves.
It has come out the other side of itself.
Which makes me wonder if I will ever
be able to recover from language enough.
Those people who pray with their palms up
as if they're catching or releasing
electromagnetic waves?
This is definitely not me. I'm following
the words as if they were closed captions
for the trumpets and blazing of the Rapture.

Venus de Milo

The moon is a bleached marble the color of the Venus de Milo.
It gets so full of itself it breaks through whole centuries.

In this twenty-first one, I am called upstairs by my grandson Noah
to see the full moon over Paris. I tell him about the centuries

inside the marble, layers and streaks. How the sculptor studies
the grain. How even then it can break out of control. Jab the chisel

too far, it leaves a white bruise. Mystery is both cool and cruel,
I'm thinking, if you stay with it, as Noah and I do on the balcony

trying to take a picture that didn't come out, that resisted us,
the way the Venus de Milo did in the afternoon, with her missing

arms, holding herself in, turning us back toward details. I explain
to Noah how rasps and rifflers are used for the final shaping. I explain

love and beauty in the language of work, what else is there to say?
Why mention how much is free-fall—accident—the combination

of genes and skill that turn them to face each other like two mirrors
making their long corridor of escape? I just climb the 64 stairs

to the balcony, panting. I say it's nothing. But then we step
into the dark and enter beauty, where there never was a foothold.

I might have told him that, but just then we were looking at the moon.

Birdhouse

Remember the year we had bluebirds there?
How they came back the next year, poked their noses
in and changed their minds? After that it was all swallows,
when we knew to clean out the twigs to get the house
ready. Swallows or wrens. Oh, they might
have been wrens, sometimes. They might have been
wrens all along, but I like the word "swallow." I think
they were swallows. That tiny slender trilling down
the scale. Wrens sound like their bodies, compact
and insistent. It was good to have either,
and their chicks. Especially their chicks, evident
only by the to-and-fro of the mothers, their fierce
judgments. It was good to have that life greet us
at the corner of the house. Bluebirds, we felt blessed.
They let us know who was in charge: blast, blast, chitter.
Also the color, the royal robes. But the swallows,
the way they swooped in and out! Who doesn't love
the word "swooped"? When they were crossing
to the trees beyond our drive, remember how we'd sit
in our kitchen chairs by the glass doors? It was so
peaceful to watch that industry, that tiny hope
carrying on, not caring a whit about us.

Talk Radio

On the conservative talk-radio show he asked me
why I write poems, since no one reads them.

I didn't like the ironic way he looked at me,
as if the two of us shared a dirty secret.

I wouldn't have a secret with him for anything.
I wouldn't tell him about the poems if he tied me up

with an American flag, how the poems and I
look at each other with deeply yearning eyes

as in the old movies that show only a bit
of flesh, a half-second shot

of a finger touching a nipple. How I get excited
at even the thought of a poem,

discouraged when inside it turns out to be
all tensed up, full of itself. How the margins say to me

in their ragged voice, "We could do this
on our lunch hour and no one would be the wiser."

Stashed / fires thrash / and brighten,
flare into blanks. I want to lick those words.

I would follow them up the dark stairs at noon.
I would never tell him how I love even

the frustration, the secret parts where rhyme upends
or comes back with an unfixable rupture, bent

words almost bleeding in their desperation to repent
and satisfy exactly, as God intended.

Fourteen Lines

The young can't understand the concept of time.
They get the way it opens like a flower, but they don't
see when it's reached the edge of itself. They don't realize
when images no longer matter, when the anecdotes that
once seemed everything lurch out front, garish as puppets.
They still believe in profound summations. When you
grow old, you believe in punctuation, in the imposition
of the period, the twin headlights of the colon, the slight
stumble of the semicolon. You look across the floor
littered with nouns and verbs the way a mother
does at the end of the day. Nothing should go on
too long. This is why you sit down and apply the period.
You are not refusing, but stopping, which is another thing.

Photo of Us on the Cottage Front Porch

We were there then, weren't we—
everything we turned out to be. I can see
signs, even though we were still inside
ourselves, thinking we could hide.

Cousin Alan hoists tiny barbells, eyes
rolled up in his head, showing only whites:
Look at me! Roger, open-faced but wry
half smile. Cousin Dennis, naked sprite

in the foreground, swimsuit hidden, poised
as if to take off, and did: all that trouble—
palsy and death. Aunt Cleone, employed
happily being the mother, seated, of boys.

And me, standing, in striped halter, arms
behind my back, watching Alan *bemusedly*—
I use that word because it charms me,
though back then I wouldn't have agreed.

I did think later—do think—the word
had always been there, and my sister has been
beside me, always, smiling nervously,
tightly holding a left-hand finger within

the right's grip. She had reason to fear,
the tumor already planted in her brain. All
of us look skinny enough to disappear,
tightly grouped off-center, as if to forestall

our own sliding to the slick white edge.

Acknowledgments

American Poetry Review: "The Purpose of Poetry";

Arts & Letters: "Dancing at Your Wedding";

Connotation Press: "Reading About the Unsolved Murders at Good Hart, Michigan, 1968";

Cortland Review: "Relationship Theory," "I Take the Boys Up the Eiffel Tower," "Chipmunk of a Rock";

Dunes Review: "Big Bang";

Flights: "Memorial Day";

The Georgia Review: "Roofers," "Talk Radio";

Image: "Note to My Sister from Notre Dame";

Kenning: "Year of the Tent Caterpillars," "Ribcage Heart," "Worms";

Miramar: "The Heart Stops," "Fourteen Lines," "Building a Cathedral," "Photo of Us on the Cottage Front Porch";

OCHO: "Bird's-Eye View," "Venus de Milo";

Poetry: "For, Or, Nor";

Prairie Schooner: "God, God" (Reprinted *PoetryDaily.com*);

Prime Numbers: "Josh, 15," "Zach, 14," "Jake, 11," "Samantha, 9," "Joie, 7," "Casey, 5," "Abigail, 3," "The Chinless Woman in the Smart Park Booth";

The Southern Review: "The Kayak and the Eiffel Tower," "Noah, 10," "Max, 9," "Rita, 6," "Felled Tree (Reprinted *PoetryDaily.com*), "Hare's Breath";

Southern Poetry Review: "The Dead," "Sugar, Sugar."

"The Kayak and the Eiffel Tower" is reprinted in *Pushcart Prize XXXIV*, 2009. "Roofers" is reprinted in *The Best American Poetry 2009*. "The Dead" is reprinted in *The Best American Poetry 2010*.

About the Author

Fleda Brown has eight previous collections of poems. Her work has twice appeared in *The Best American Poetry* and has won a Pushcart Prize, the Felix Pollak Prize, the Philip Levine Prize, the Great Lakes Colleges New Writer's Award, and has twice been a finalist for the National Poetry Series. Her latest collection of essays, with Vermont poet laureate Sydney Lea, *Growing Old in Poetry: Two Poets, Two Lives*, was published in 2013, exclusively on Kindle by Autumn House Books, Pittsburgh, PA. Her memoir, *Driving With Dvorak*, was published in 2010 by the University of Nebraska Press. She has also coedited an anthology of Delaware writers and a collection of essays on D. H. Lawrence. She is professor emerita at the University of Delaware, and poet laureate of Delaware, 2001–2007. She now lives with her husband, Jerry Beasley, in Traverse City, Michigan, not far from their cottage on Intermediate Lake. She is on the faculty of the Rainier Writing Workshop, a low-residency MFA program in Tacoma, Washington.

BOA Editions, Ltd.
American Poets Continuum Series

Colophon

BOA Editions, Ltd., a not-for-profit publisher of poetry and other literary works, fosters readership and appreciation of contemporary literature. By identifying, cultivating, and publishing both new and established poets and selecting authors of unique literary talent, BOA brings high-quality literature to the public. Support for this effort comes from the sale of its publications, grant funding, and private donations.

*

The publication of this book is made possible, in part, by the special support of the following individuals:

Anonymous
Jeanne Marie Beaumont
Bernadette Catalana
Anne Germanacos
Michael S. Glaser
X. J. & Dorothy M. Kennedy
Laurie Kutchins
Barbara & John Lovenheim
Peter & Phyllis Makuck
Werner K. & Charles G. Postler
Boo Poulin
Steven O. Russell & Phyllis Rifkin-Russell
David W. Ryon
Michael Waters & Mihaela Moscaliuc